TABLE OF CONTENTS

Introduction

Reading books is a favourite activity of many people in their free time. When we are reading, we live in another world. A new life opens, there will be no more complication, difficulty or grief that real life brings about. We live naturally like kids with different feelings such as happy, upset, angry... During the process of reading a book, we can collect a lot of useful knowledge. So, reading book is a good habit that parents should encourage our children to practice to have even when they are very young.

There are many kinds of book, which are suitable for people all of age and satisfy the knowledge need. If the kids are the kind of people who love to explore the world, let them read science books, these books will explain all secrets of the universe. If they like traveling, handbooks will take you to the beautiful land that you haven't been to and give you valuable experiences.

Anyway, if they just want to entertain after a long tiring day at school, a riddle or trivia or a joke book is an interesting choice. It so wonderful, right? I think that not just to me but all of us, reading books is a meaningful activity and everyone should have this habit.

QUIZ 1

1. This is a vehicle that has wheels and flies too. But it is not an aircraft. What vehicle is it?
2. I have a big family. My mother is the cloud. My father is the wind. My sons are the streams and rivers. My daughters are the seas and oceans. I finally rest on Earth. What am I?
3. I only respond when spoken to. I don't speak on my own. What am I?
4. A man was carrying wood on this head, which was neither straight nor crooked. What kind of wood was it?
5. This turns all things around and does it without moving. What is it?
6. I put it up and it is bright. I put it down and it is dark.
7. One night, a king with his queen went to his place, which was completely empty. There was no one inside the palace or the courtyard or anywhere else. Yet, the next morning, three people came riding out of the palace. How?
8. How many different kinds of species of animals and birds and plants did Moses take on his beautiful Ark?
9. There is water running down a hill. When will it stop?
10. I am a 6-letter word and I am secure and strong. Take away the head and I become an eating or meeting place. Take away the head again and I am ready's partner. Put both my heads back and I become an animal shelter.

ANSWERS QUIZ 1

1. A garbage truck
2. Rain
3. An echo
4. Sawdust
5. Counterfeit money
6. Light switch
7. Because the people who rode in were the (k)night, the king and his queen!
8. None. It was not Moses' Ark. It was Noah's.
9. When the water reaches the bottom
10. Stable

QUIZ 2

1. Sometimes my tines are long and sometimes they are short. But my tines end before my report is submitted. What am I?
2. The higher I go, the hotter I get. I am stuck in my glass cage. What am I?
3. Which part of London can you find in France?
4. I am at the start of the end, I am in every second and every minute, and I am the end of life too.
5. I am a word that has to be pronounced wrong.
6. A little boy was climbing down a 25-foot ladder and suddenly he fell down. But the boy was not hurt. How is it possible?
7. This vegetable is very bad for ships. Which one?
8. I have four fingers and a thumb just like you. And yet I am not alive. My partner is just like me; all fingers but no life. What am I?
9. This has a jacket but never wears trousers.
10. I bring about darkness even I force open an opening. The hyena, hippo and the horse know me, but spiders and snails don't know me. What am I?

ANSWERS QUIZ 2

1. Lightning
2. Mercury (in a thermometer)
3. The letter N
4. The letter E
5. The word 'wrong'
6. He was on the last step when he fell down
7. A leek (leak)
8. A glove (right and left gloves)
9. Book
10. A yawn

QUIZ 3

1. It runs and runs and does not ever stop. You can sometimes see it, but it never sees. It brings boredom when it is long and fear when it is short.
2. I am black seeds on white land. I see things.
3. I have a thousand needles and yet I cannot sew or stitch.
4. This brave goose fights with snakes. Which one?
5. This has been around us for millions of years and yet it is not more than one month old.
6. This group of three has one who sits and never gets up, the second who eats whatever you feed him, and the third who goes up never to return.
7. It has an eye that cannot see on one end and the other end is sharp
8. If you happen to know me, then I feel like nothing. But if you don't know me, I can be puzzling.
9. Audrey's mother has 2 sons and 2 daughters. Her sons' names are John and Philip and one of her daughters is called Margaret. What is this lady's second daughter's name?
10. You can actually put something into a wooden box and still make it lighter than before. What can you put?

ANSWERS QUIZ 3

1. Time
2. An eye
3. Porcupine
4. A mongoose
5. Moon
6. Stove, fire, and smoke
7. Needle
8. A riddle or puzzle
9. Audrey
10. You can put holes

QUIZ 4

1. The electric train is traveling in a southwesterly direction and a northeasterly wind is blowing in the area. Which direction is the smoke from the train traveling?
2. This is something that can be heard but can never be seen or caught.
3. Is there a law against a man to marry his widow's sister?
4. I am the letter that can change your story into a building. Which letter am I?
5. Which creature walks on 4 legs in the morning, 2 legs in the afternoon, and 3 legs at night?
6. I am this juicy fruit that can be red, green, or yellow
7. Name two perennial veggies that can grow for several years after you have planted them once unlike other veggies, which have to be replanted every year.
8. Tim is alone in his house at night. The lights are off and it is so dark that nothing is visible. Yet, Tim is lying on the couch and reading a book. How is it possible?
9. A man drives his car all the way to the bank and shouts out loud, 'I am bankrupt.' Why does he do it?
10. Everyone loves to give this away. Many people need it too. However, rarely do people use it themselves. What is it?

ANSWERS QUIZ 4

1. No smoke from an electric train
2. Remark
3. Only half the way; because when he is on the other half of the field, he is running out of the field
4. E (story becomes storey)
5. Man: crawls as a baby, walks on two when he is youthful, and uses a stick when he is old
6. Apple
7. Rhubarb and asparagus
8. Tim is blind and his book is written in 'Braille'
9. Because he is playing the game, Monopoly
10. Advice

QUIZ 5

1. Even the most intelligent people will overlook this thing. What?
2. A microbe colony was founded by a single cell at around noon. This healthy microbe colony is lying in a petri dish. Every minute, each of the microbes is dividing into two. At exactly 12:33, the petri dish gets half full. At what time will the petri dish get completely full?
3. This thing is so delicate that simply naming it can break it. What are we talking about?
4. Unlike a knife that gets blunter with more use, I get sharper with more use. What am I?
5. In the morning I lose my head but always get it back in the night. What am I?
6. What is the difference between a watchmaker and a jailer?
7. I am full of puzzles. Some people have managed to solve some of my puzzles and yet there are millions more left to the solved. I am both adored and feared.
8. Rolling cars, rising railroads, roaring lions! Can you spell that without any Rs?
9. I am all around the wood but not a bit of me is inside. What am I?
10. I carry a lot of memories, but none of them are mine.

ANSWERS QUIZ 5

1. Their nose
2. The wise man simply told them to switch the camels.
3. Silence
4. Your brain
5. A pillow
6. The watchmaker sells watches while the jailer watches his cells
7. Math
8. Yes, T-H-A-T. It has no Rs!
9. Bark of a tree
10. A photo frame

QUIZ 6

1. I am a natural pathway that is located between high natural masses and if you remove one letter from me, you have an artificial pathway between manmade masses. What am I?
2. The more you have of me, the more difficult it is for you to see. What am I?
3. With a sunny and yellow disposition, I have a black eye in the middle. I am attached strongly down and yet follow my king as he moves around. What am I?
4. This alphabet is the longest of all. Which one?
5. If everyone in the country bought white cars, what will we become?
6. My face is full of numbers and yet you will not find thirteen. What am I?
7. I am as light as a feather. I am, in fact, lighter than air. Yet, the strongest man in this world cannot lift me. Who am I?
8. You need the following things to start a fire: petrol or kerosene or paper or candle and a matchbox along with a bit of cotton wool. What will you light first?
9. The answer to this question may be yes, but it actually means no. What is the question?
10. What has two head, six legs, two hands, and four ears? Remember it walks only on four legs.

ANSWERS QUIZ 6

1. Valley
2. Darkness
3. A sunflower
4. Q (queue)
5. A white carnation
6. A clock
7. A bubble
8. Because the population of China is far greater than that of Japan
9. Do you mind?
10. A rider on horse

QUIZ 7

1. You can enter it, but you cannot live on it. What am I talking about?
2. I am weak and strong too. I have little powers and yet I am powerful.
3. I am a word of three letters that means a little. You add two letters and I become even littler. What word am I?
4. With no arms, no feet, no wings, I still can climb towards the skies. What am I?
5. There are 12 people running a race and you have just managed to overtake the boy who was running in the 4th position. What is your position now?
6. What falls down but is unbreakable?
7. To use me, you have to do this: Throw away the outside; cook the inside. Then eat the outside and throw away the inside.
8. I come where the rainbow ends and water begins.
9. There is one way a leopard can change its spots. How?
10. This thing is some distance away. It is possible to see it and move towards it. Yet, the distance will always remain. What is it?

ANSWERS QUIZ 7

1. The 'enter' key on the keyboard
2. Emotions
3. Few
4. Smoke
5. Fourth
6. Night (nightfall)
7. Corn
8. The letter 'w'
9. By moving from spot to spot
10. A glove

QUIZ 8

1. Teddy bears never ever feel hungry. Why?
2. We put this on the table and cut it many times. Yet, it cannot be eaten. What is it?
3. I have no wings and yet I can soar. I can be wild and crazy. I can frighten even the strongest man. (Clue: I cannot be touched)
4. Although I don't have ears, eyes, tongue, or nose, I can hear, see, taste, and smell everything? Who is this all-in-one?
5. It is as round as a ring and so deep that even all the horses of the king cannot pull it up. However, it has something sweet at the bottom that you can pull up. What is it?
6. Which moves faster: heat or cold?
7. Take away the head, it goes higher. Put the head, it goes lower.
8. I have no siblings and yet, this man's father is my father's son. Who are we talking about?
9. I am lighter than a feather and yet the strongest man in this world cannot hold me for more than a minute or two. What am I?
10. This creature is alive without breathing. It is as cold as death. It is never thirsty and yet is always drinking. What is it?

ANSWERS QUIZ 8

1. Because they are stuffed
2. A pack of cards
3. Imagination
4. Your brain
5. A well of water
6. Heat; because everyone can catch a cold
7. Pillow
8. The man himself
9. Breath
10. Fish

QUIZ 9

1. Two ladies were standing facing opposite directions. One was facing east and the other was facing west. Yet, they were able to see each other. How is it possible

2. Black when clean; white when dirty; what is it?

3. This is round as a ring and flat as a leaf. It has two or four eyes but cannot see at all. What am I?

4. With beautiful white fleece, I follow Mary everywhere she goes. I can be eaten too

5. She had just learned to drive. She went down on a one-way street and was seen by the cop and yet he did not penalize her. How?

6. Everyone has this dress. But no one can wear it.

7. I am a small house full of meat. I have no door or window for you to get in. You will have to break my walls down for that.

8. Using only 8's, how can you get 1000 as the total? You can only add. You cannot subtract or multiply or divide.

9. You take this away from there and it comes here. What is it you take away?

10. I cover your body, but I am not your clothes. The more you use me the thinner I get and the cleaner you get. What am I?

ANSWERS QUIZ 9

1. They were holding mirrors
2. Blackboard
3. Button
4. A lamb
5. Because the new driver was walking down the one-way street
6. Address
7. A nut
8. $888+88+8+8+8 = 1000$
9. The letter 'T'
10. Bar of soap

QUIZ 10

1. Which insect is the best at gaming?
2. Steve is in an open field with a ball in his hand. He throws the ball as hard as he can without bouncing it on any surface. After a few seconds, the ball comes right back to him. How is it possible?
3. Most people hate me but some people like me. I can change appearances and no matter how much you try to hide me, I will end up showing. I can never ever go down. What am I?
4. I love hot water and I keep the water hot for a long time.
5. A man and his son were involved in an accident and were taken to two different hospitals. The son's doctor looked at him and said, "I cannot operate on this boy because he is my son." How is this possible?
6. Steve is a huge football fan. He is so crazy about the game that he claims that he can tell the score even before the game starts. How is it possible?
7. Always full when you see her and yet nothing comes out of her, she is white, round, and beautiful.
8. The one who makes me doesn't use me at the time he makes me. The one who pays the money to buy me does not need it for himself. The one who uses me doesn't even know he is using me.
9. You have to add 20 to the number 100. How many times can you do it?
10. The power hat is given to me when the king is dead. The hat that is put on my head is very difficult to carry. Who am I?

ANSWERS QUIZ 10

1. A cricket
2. He throws the ball in the upward direction
3. Age
4. Hot water bottle
5. Because the doctor was the mother of the boy
6. You will light the match first
7. Full moon
8. Coffin
9. Only once; because after that 100 will become 120
10. Prince

QUIZ 11

1. It has a bark, but it cannot bite at all.
2. This musical instrument is something you can only hear but never touch or see. Which is it?
3. There are three bulbs in the upstairs room and their corresponding switches are on the ground floor. Now, you need to identify which switch is for which bulb. The restriction is you can climb up the stairs only once to check. However, you can put on or off a switch any number of times and for any duration of time. How will you identify which switch is connected to which bulb?
4. Yellow bricks are used to build yellow houses. Red bricks are used to build red houses. Blue bricks are used to build blue houses. What color bricks will be used to build a green house?
5. A man living in the US cannot be buried in the United Kingdom because ______________
6. This thing is most often full the entire day and empty always at night. What is it?
7. This thing is rarely used in the day. It cries right through the night and sometimes dies by the time the morning comes. What is it?
8. I am a word that means hardly there. If you take away my head, I become a great-smelling herb used in cooking.
9. What can hold water despite being full of holes?
10. I am fine and powerful. I can build castles. I can bring down mountains. I can blind people and yet help a few people to see.

ANSWERS QUIZ 11

1. Tree
2. Your voice
3. All the other tools are red herrings. Simply pour water into the pipe until the ball floats up to the top.
4. A green house is always made of glass
5. The North Pole
6. Your shoes
7. A candle
8. Sparsely (parsley)
9. Sponge
10. Sand

QUIZ 12

1. Name an honest musical instrument.
2. A dog runs into a field at great speed. How far can he run into the field?
3. Although water is life on this earth, that is the one thing that will kill me almost immediately.
4. This has no middle, no end, no beginning. And it's simply delicious too.
5. This fellow is my best friend because he is always there to take care of my mistakes. Who is he?
6. The yolk of an egg is white or the yolk of an egg are white?
7. I come once in a month, twice in a fortnight, but never in a hundred years. What am I?
8. Three men were rowing in a boat when suddenly there came a big storm and the boat capsized. Two men got their hair all wet. The third did not. How?
9. This comes in green too. But it is not a leaf. It copies others, but it is not a monkey. What is it?
10. Is an old five-dollar note more than valuable than a new one?

ANSWERS QUIZ 12

1. An upright piano
2. Everyone knows that before any game starts, the score is always 0-0
3. Fire
4. Doughnut
5. An eraser
6. Neither. Yolk is not white
7. The letter 'T'
8. He was bald
9. A parrot
10. Of course, $5 is always worthier than $1 (new one)

QUIZ 13

1. This only goes up and never comes down; no matter what.
2. You have drawn a line on a paper. Your friend comes and does something to make this line bigger. However, she does not touch or make changes to your line in any way. How did she do it?
3. I always promise to come but never am today.
4. My handbag is 35 cm in height and 40 cm in length. I have removed everything from it and it is now totally empty. I have coins measuring 2 cm in diameter. How many such coins can I put into my empty handbag?
5. We are brothers who make something whole and yet we never meet. Who are we?
6. This thing is not alive, has no lungs, and yet needs air for survival. What is it?
7. I am the most slippery nation in this entire world. Which country am I?
8. I am loaded with keys of varying sizes and shapes and yet none of them can be used to open a single door. What am I?
9. Steve puts his hand into his pocket. It has nothing and is totally empty. Yet, Steve finds something. What does he find in his empty pocket?
10. This thing flies all around and all day but still never leaves its place. (Clue: People sometimes sing a special song as it flies around)

ANSWERS QUIZ 13

1. Your age
2. She drew a line that is shorter than your line next to it.
3. Tomorrow
4. Only one; because when you put in the first one, the handbag is no longer empty!
5. Day and night
6. Your fingers
7. Greece.
8. A piano
9. A hole
10. Flag

QUIZ 14

1. What do bees say to flowers?
2. This letter is an important part of your head. Which alphabet is it?
3. I am thin and beautiful. My roots are on top. I love the winters and hate the summers. A single ray of sunshine can kill me. What am I?
4. I have four legs and a flat face. People use me always yet I never tire. I am always ready for work whenever you are. I usually have another 4-legged partner
5. The Wilson family were very wealthy and lived in a huge, beautifully done up, circular home. Mr. Wilson was a stickler for cleanliness. He woke up one morning and found a stain of jam on the table. He spoke to everyone. I was playing basketball – said little Wilson. I was sewing in my room – said Mrs. Wilson I was dusting the corners the house – said the maid. Who was lying?
6. This boy had a wonderful red flashlight that burned quite bright. But one day, he buried it. Why did he do that?
7. This question can never get a response of yes.
8. I look and act like a cat. But I am not a cat. What am I?
9. This alphabet is the wettest of all. Which alphabet is it?
10. Round and small, I am served at a table by two or four. I am hit back and forth and you will love me.

ANSWERS QUIZ 14

1. Hey, honey!
2. I (eye)
3. An icicle
4. Desk
5. The maid. There are no corners in a circular home
6. Because the batteries died
7. Are you sleeping?
8. Kitten
9. C
10. Ping pong ball

QUIZ 15

1. Name this thing: it has 'kst' in the center, in (at the start) and (at the very end)
2. A crook brought me a coin, which had an embossing on it saying it was made in 200 B.C. I knew immediately this was a fake. How did I know?
3. I fly without wings and I cry without tears. Who am I?
4. This is the name of an insect. The first part of this insect is another insect. What are the two insects being spoken of?
5. This is a room that no one can enter and there is always no room here. What kind of room can this be?
6. You will always find me meandering outside whether rain or shine. I never once step inside any house.
7. You have 20 apples and 13 girls to distribute equally among. How will you do it in such a way that no girl gets more or less? The apples are equally distributed.
8. April showers bring flowers. What do May flowers bring?
9. A window cleaner was working on the 45th floor of an apartment building cleaning windows there. He suddenly fell down but was unhurt. How?
10. This thing binds two people and yet touches one only.

ANSWERS QUIZ 15

1. Inkstand (kst in the middle, in (at the beginning), and (at the end)
2. The concept of B.C, (Before Christ) came into being only after Christ was born. How did the people know about B.C. during that time?
3. Clouds
4. Beetle
5. This is not a legal question. If his wife is a widow, isn't he dead and if he is dead, where is the question of marriage
6. Street
7. Simple; make apple juice and divide the juice equally among the 13 girls
8. Pilgrims (the ship Mayflower)
9. Because he was cleaning the windows from the inside of a home and he merely slipped on a drop of water and fell down on the floor. He got up and continued cleaning
10. A wedding ring

QUIZ 16

1. I have legs, a strong back and two good arms as well. Yet, I don't walk nor move around. What am I?
2. I make things tight from one direction and make them loose from another direction. I turn and turn until the end is reached.
3. I run all around the city or home and yet I am unmoving.
4. I can be seen in water. But I never get wet.
5. You can whip and beat this thing until it becomes hard. Yet it will not shed a single tear.
6. When you break me, there is no noise.
7. Numbers 88, 69 and 11 have something in common. Can you see it?
8. The ages of a father and his son total to 66. The numbers representing the ages of the father and son are reversed. What are their ages? (Clue: There are more than one answer to this riddle)
9. You need me to move forward. The more you move forward, the more of me you leave behind.
10. A ladder is overhanging on the side of the ship. It has 20 rungs and the bottom-most one is just about touching the sea. There is a gap of 20 cm between every pair of rungs. Now, the tide rises at the rate 15 cm. When will the 6th rung (from the top) get fully submerged in water?

ANSWERS QUIZ 16

1. An armchair
2. Screwdriver
3. Wall
4. Your reflection
5. Cream
6. Promise
7. All three of them look the same upside down as well
8. Any of the following three will be taken as the right answer: 60+6, 51+15, 42+24
9. Footsteps
10. Never, if the rising tide is lifting the ladder, it is also lifting the ship at the same rate.

QUIZ 17

1. I am found all over the world. I may be quite thin, but I am very important. You need me to learn. My parents are the forests. What am I?

2. You are sitting on the bridge watching a boat filled with people coming towards the shore. As it comes slowly, you realize that there is not one single person on the boat. How is it possible?

3. Who is the most silent Member of Parliament?

4. What has plenty of teeth but never bothers to brush them?

5. You are late returning from work and there is a power shutdown in your locality. Your home is dark and looks eerie. You fumble through your handbag and find a cigar, a small portable kerosene lamp, and a matchbox. You open the door and the room is cold as ever though the fireplace is filled with fresh wood. What will you light first?

6. The more it dries, the more it gets wet. What is it?

7. How can an island and the letter T be compared? Why are they both similar to each other?

8. You also have them and use them to wring with woe, hoe a row, and slay a foe.

9. I am my father's child and my mother's child. But I am no one' son.

10. A squirrel, a bird, and a monkey are sitting on top of a coconut tree. A giraffe is standing close by too with its long neck ready to eat the banana. Which of the four will reach the banana first?

ANSWERS QUIZ 17

1. Paper
2. All the people on the boat are married men and women.
3. The letter 'I' because it is not pronounced in 'parliament'
4. Piano
5. A matchstick
6. A towel
7. Both are in the middle of waTer.
8. Hands
9. A daughter
10. Bananas don't come in coconut trees!

QUIZ 18

1. Two boys were born to the same mother at the same time, the same day, and the same year. Yet, these two boys were not twins. How is it possible?

2. This question gets you different answers right through the day. Yet, all the answers are correct. What is the question?

3. I have three full feet and yet I cannot walk or run or play. What am I?

4. It is round and short at the beginning and the end and high in the center.

5. Your school and your eyes have something in common. Can you guess what it is?

6. I am used for drinking coffee. I am also a stop and can make others stop.

7. I may have a red hat and a stony heart. But I am still lovable.

8. This has roots that no one can or has seen. It is taller than trees. It keeps on moving upwards and yet it does not grow. What is it?

9. Even though I have innumerable legs, I cannot stand straight. I have to only lean. You make me dirty so you can feel squeaky clean. What am I?

10. Whoever makes these things does not tell, those who don't know these things will take it, and those who know about these things will not touch it with a barge pole. What are we talking about?

ANSWERS QUIZ 18

1. They were two of triplets
2. What time is it?
3. A yardstick
4. Ohio
5. Pupils
6. Brake/break
7. Cherry
8. A mountain
9. A broom
10. Your eyes

QUIZ 19

1. You have two jugs of capacities 5 and 3 gallons each respectively. You have no other vessel or measuring device. How will you measure out 4 gallons from this setup?
2. Anybody can catch this. But no one can throw it. What is it?
3. I can run down a slope easily. However, I cannot walk. What or who am I?
4. The name of this king begins and ends with five hundred. Five is right in the middle. First of all numbers and the first of all alphabets take up either place of the exact middle. Combine everything and you get a name that is the name of a great king. Name the king.
5. This animal can jump higher than a castle. Which one?
6. I pass right through the sun and yet do not make a shadow.
7. This thing has many eyes and yet it cannot see. What is it?
8. It remains only with me as long as I don't share it. Once I share it, it is not mine anymore. What is this?
9. Imagine you are in a dark and dingy room and suddenly you hear eerie noises. You also red eyes and teeth like that of the vampire you read in the story yesterday. The door is locked from outside. There are no other doors or windows. How will you get out?
10. We are family of 12. I come second and yet I am the smallest. How is it possible?

ANSWERS QUIZ 19

1. Fill the five-gallon vessel completely. Then, pour out two gallons from here into the 3-gallon vessel and then throw it out. After this, pour the leftover two gallons from the bigger vessel into the three-gallon vessel. Next, pour enough water into the big vessel so that it is completely full again. Now, you will have one gallon of space in the smaller vessel. Pour enough water from the big vessel to completely fill the small one. This will leave exactly four gallons in the big vessel.
2. A cold
3. Water
4. DAVID
5. All animals can jump higher than a castle because a castle cannot jump
6. The wind
7. A hole
8. A secret
9. Just stop imagining
10. The family is the 12 months of the year. February has the least number of days and therefore the smallest.

QUIZ 20

1. Four children, a dog, and the mother of the four children were walking holding a small little umbrella. Yet, none of them got wet. How?

2. I am a very lonely word and I am 5 letters long. You take away one letter and I am still lonely and if you take away another letter, I am still solitary. What word am I?

3. With lots of eyes and round or oval-shaped, I am loved by nearly everyone in this world. You can boil me or cut me into pieces and fry me and I turn out yummy.

4. When I am young, I'm sweet. In my middle age, I am better. But when I am old, I'm the best.

5. I am something very closely related to everything in this world. I only move forward and there is no going back for me. What am I?

6. I have feet but no legs to speak of. Who or what am I?

7. This has a horn but cannot honk. What is it?

8. How many oranges and apples can you put into an empty bag?

9. This alphabet can be very, very hot. Which one?

10. Five men were on the road. Four were walking at the same speed and the fifth one was not. Yet, they all reached the destination at the same time. What is being described?

ANSWERS QUIZ 20

1. Because it was not raining
2. Alone
3. Potatoes
4. Wine
5. Age
6. A snail
7. A rhino
8. Only one; because after the first one is put, the bag is not empty any more
9. T (tea)
10. Four pall-bearers carrying a coffin